IMAGES
of America

# NORTH CLACKAMAS

The Float of All Nations is pictured during a July 4th celebration in Milwaukie in 1907. (Clackamas County Historical Society.)

**ON THE COVER:** This image shows school buses at the Milwaukie Grammar School in the 1920s. In 1925, Milwaukie—along with Clackamas, Oak Grove, Concord, and other grade schools— was consolidated to form a new high school district called "Union." This was a step toward the formation of the North Clackamas School District in 1971. (Milwaukie Museum.)

IMAGES
*of America*

# NORTH
# CLACKAMAS

Mark W. Hurlburt

ARCADIA
PUBLISHING

Published by Arcadia Publishing
Charleston, South Carolina

Printed in the United States of America

Library of Congress Control Number: 2021939291

For all general information, please contact Arcadia Publishing:
Telephone 843-853-2070
Fax 843-853-0044
E-mail sales@arcadiapublishing.com
For customer service and orders:
Toll-Free 1-888-313-2665

Visit us on the Internet at www.arcadiapublishing.com

*To Frankie*

# CONTENTS

# ACKNOWLEDGMENTS

I would like to thank Mrs. McFarlane, my Clackamas High School history teacher, for inspiring me to love exploring history, and Karin Morey, my "Jedi Master," for mentoring me in local history. The images in this book appear courtesy of the Clackamas County Historical Society (CCHS), the Wilmer Gardner Research Library (WGRL), the Milwaukie Museum (MM), Chris Guntermann of the Baker Cabin Historical Society (BCHS), Kandi Ho of North Clackamas Parks and Recreation District (NCPRD), Kay Mordock, Trena Heydel, and the Happy Valley History Collection (HVHC). Information for some of the photographs of Oak Grove and Jennings Lodge was provided by Mike Schmeer of Oak Lodge History Detectives. I would also like to thank Judy Chambers, Adrian Wegner, Jo Lynn Dow, Richard Craven, Sandy McGuire, Steve Dietz, David Aschenbrenner, and Greg Hemer for their contributions in helping create this book.

# INTRODUCTION

The region of North Clackamas comprises the northern part of Clackamas County, Oregon. Clackamas County was formed as one of the four original districts (or counties) of the Oregon Provisional Government on July 5, 1843. The county was named after the Native Americans who lived in the region south of the Columbia River down to Willamette Falls and east of the Willamette River to the foothills of the Cascade Mountains. At its greatest extent, the region of North Clackamas begins in the north at the border between Multnomah and Clackamas Counties and stretches the same distance south to the Clackamas River. The Willamette River forms its western boundary, and it extends eastward beyond Damascus toward the town of Boring. Since the late 20th century, North Clackamas has been one of the most monumentally changed regions in Oregon. This book will present a glimpse at what the region used to look like.

The communities and areas of North Clackamas have been linked together since at least the early 20th century, when residents considered seceding from the rest of the county. In 1908, J.P. Shaw of the *Milwaukie Record* newspaper advocated for the formation of a new county by combining eastern Multnomah and northern Clackamas Counties, with Milwaukie as the county seat. A meeting of northern Clackamas County residents was held in Oak Grove in February 1910 to discuss secession and annexing their region into Multnomah County. Advocates wanted to annex into Multnomah to take advantage of the county's lower tax rates. Property owners in the North Clackamas area, described at the time as living mostly north of the Clackamas River and east of the Willamette River, believed their property values would increase, and they could use City of Portland tax funds to improve local roads. The plan faced opposition from the rest of Clackamas County and from Multnomah County, as annexing the North Clackamas region would significantly increase the size of Multnomah. This meant the costs of improving roads and maintaining bridges would increase and create higher taxes for current Multnomah County citizens.

In 1920, Harvey G. Starkweather, an Oak Grove area resident, was among the proponents of the secession of North Clackamas to Multnomah County. He argued that it would be beneficial to the development of Portland, with the annexed area providing homes for Portland businessmen and workers. The plan showed strong support among North Clackamas residents, with one meeting at Milwaukie's city hall favoring secession by a vote of 74 to 23. The fight went to the state legislature, but the secessionists ultimately failed. Although the plan to secede was not successful, the communities of northern Clackamas County being linked together as "North Clackamas" became a well-known identity.

Local newspaper publishers used North Clackamas in the names of their publications. In 1922, George A. McArthur began publishing the *North Clackamas News* in Milwaukie. The paper began as the *Milwaukie Press* in 1916 and temporarily ceased publication in 1921. Shortly after McArthur restarted the paper under the new name, the *Gladstone Reporter* moved to Oak Grove and changed its name to the *North Clackamas Reporter*. To avoid confusion, the *North Clackamas News* changed its name to the *Milwaukie Review* and marketed itself as "the successor to the *North Clackamas News*." Over the 20th century, the paper changed owners, names, and locations several times before eventually becoming known as the *Clackamas Review*.

In the early 1970s, the *Clackamas Review* played a pivotal role in the consolidation of local schools into the North Clackamas School District. At the time, the North Clackamas area had separate elementary school districts and one unified high school district. Proponents believed a single unified school district would bring more efficient administration, save money, and provide a better quality of education for all. But not everyone loved the proposal, and it faced opposition. As the unification was being discussed, *Review* editor and reporter Jeb Bladine interviewed parents and two teachers at the Concord School District who shared concerns about the district's superintendent. When the superintendent found out about the meeting, he fired the two teachers. Bladine wrote his article, and Concord voters wanted to oust the superintendent. They achieved this by overwhelmingly voting to consolidate, and the measure carried.

Earlier, in the 1920s, North Clackamas communities worked together to create a unified high school district to provide a close-to-home option for students wanting higher education after grammar school. Union High School District No. 5 was formed by a vote of the people from the districts involved on February 28, 1925. This new district united the grammar school districts of Milwaukie, Concord, Rock Creek, Harmony, Battin, Clackamas, East Clackamas, Sunnyside, East Mount Scott, Oak Grove, and Wichita. A bond election held on May 9, 1925, passed, and the construction of a new high school building commenced. The new Union High School in Milwaukie was dedicated on September 3, 1926.

Decades later, after voters approved the creation of the North Clackamas School District, the adoption of a final plan for this district, also known as administrative school district No. 12, was approved by the Clackamas County District Boundary Board on September 20, 1971. The new district united the former grade school districts of Milwaukie, Concord, Clackamas, and Oak Grove, as well as the Union High School district in Milwaukie. According to the 1970 federal census, the population of the area that would comprise school district No. 12 was 58,628.

In addition to the North Clackamas School District, there have been numerous organizations and groups that have adopted the name "North Clackamas" over the years; these have included various portions of the region described at its greatest extent. In 1990, voters approved the formation of the North Clackamas Parks and Recreation District to provide services and facilities to local communities. The North Clackamas Chamber of Commerce was established to promote and support local businesses. The popular aquatic park bearing the name has served as a place for children to learn how to swim and as a major attraction in North Clackamas since it opened in 1994. Summer softball teams like the North Clackamas Ice and Royals unified high school players from the North Clackamas School District. These are just a few examples.

The boundaries of the North Clackamas region have differed over the years between the school district, chamber of commerce, and parks and recreation district. The focus of this book will cover the area mostly served by the school district, which includes the cities of Milwaukie and Happy Valley and their surrounding communities and areas. The purpose of this book is not to be a complete visual history or to tell the specific stories of the cities and communities of North Clackamas, as individual books could be written to offer a much more detailed history of each of the areas covered in this book. The intent behind this book is to present an introduction to the history of the North Clackamas region and inspire interest in those wanting to know more about local stories through research or by supporting local historical organizations.

# One

# THE REGION OF NORTH CLACKAMAS

At its greatest extent, the North Clackamas region stretches from its northern boundary—at the border between Multnomah and Clackamas Counties—to as far south as the Clackamas River. This photograph looking east shows Milwaukie Bay in the 1940s at the region's western boundary along the Willamette River with Mount Hood in the background. (MM.)

This 1948 map of the North Clackamas area shows many of the communities, school locations, roads, and notable features of the region. It shows the locations of several old schools, including Battin, Harmony, Concord, East Clackamas, Sunnyside, East Mount Scott, Carver, and Union. Eighty-Second Street (today's Eighty-Second Avenue and Highway 213), near the left center of the map, roughly divides the west and east sides of the region as explored in this book. "U.S.A.

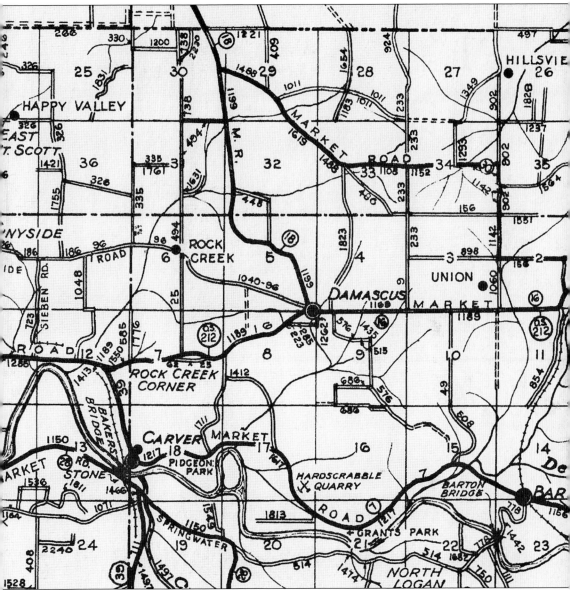

"Barracks" refers to the location of Camp Withycombe in Clackamas. The Willamette River, on the left side of the map, marks the western boundary of the North Clackamas region. The Clackamas River roughly marks the southern boundary, and the Clackamas County border with Multnomah County marks the northern boundary. (MM.)

The Cedar Crossing Covered Bridge, shown here in a 1987 photograph by Happy Valley photographer Bud Unruh, could be considered the "gateway" into North Clackamas. It is located near the border between Clackamas and Multnomah Counties, which forms the northern boundary for the region. Deardorff Road, named after the first non-Indigenous family to settle in Happy Valley, winds like a snake southward into the city of Happy Valley. (HVHC.)

The Willamette River, shown here at Milwaukie around 1970, forms the western boundary of North Clackamas. A north-flowing river, it traverses the Willamette Valley and cascades over Willamette Falls, one of the largest waterfalls in the United States. The North Clackamas communities that have banks along its waters include Milwaukie, Oak Grove, and Jennings Lodge. (MM.)

The eastern boundary of the North Clackamas region reaches beyond Damascus toward the town of Boring. The Union School in Damascus was established in the 1880s and located on the northern side of what is now Highway 212 in eastern Damascus. In 1921, the original school was replaced with a new school south of the highway on the site where Damascus Middle School would later be built. (WGRL.)

The Clackamas River forms what can be considered the southern boundary of the North Clackamas region. It flows across Clackamas County until it reaches the Willamette River at Gladstone. This undated photograph shows the Clackamas River with the Gladstone railroad bridge in the background. (CCHS.)

Members of the Clackamas tribe lived in the area south of the Columbia River down to Willamette Falls and east of the Willamette River to the foothills of the Cascade Mountains. They were part of the Chinookan language group of Native Americans, and their descendants belong to the Confederated Tribes of the Grand Ronde. This illustration shows the interior of a Chinookan plank house as it appeared during the Charles Wilkes expedition in the early 1840s. (CCHS.)

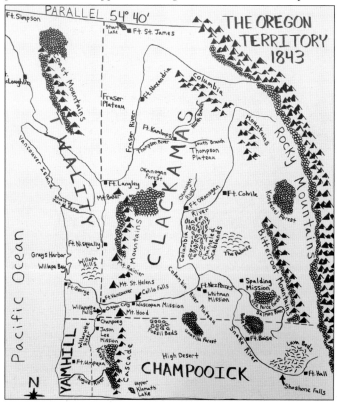

North Clackamas is a region of Clackamas County, which began as one of the four original "districts" of the Oregon Provisional Government in 1843 along with Champooick, Twality, and Yamhill. The Clackamas District stretched as far east as what is now western Montana and as far north as British Columbia. Over the years, its boundaries shrunk due to the establishment of new counties and state borders. (WGRL.)

In 1920, Oak Grove area resident Harvey Gordon Starkweather was a leader in the effort to get North Clackamas to secede from the rest of Clackamas County and be annexed to Multnomah County. Although the plan to secede was not successful, the communities of northern Clackamas County being referred to as "North Clackamas" became a well-known identity. Starkweather was a son of William and Eliza Starkweather, Oregon pioneers who made their home on land where McLoughlin Boulevard was later built. The nearby Concord School received its name from a suggestion made by William. Harvey's father served in the Oregon territorial legislature and Harvey's uncle, Harvey Gordon, designed Oregon's state seal. Harvey Gordon Starkweather was a teacher and a superintendent of Clackamas County. He was also a farmer and married Mary Alice Risley, a daughter of pioneer Jacob Risley, who settled in the area. Starkweather was also a local leader in the Democratic Party and in the Society of Sons and Daughters of Oregon Pioneers. (MM.)

Since the 1950s, the North Clackamas Chamber of Commerce has worked to promote and advocate for cities and unincorporated communities of the North Clackamas region by providing avenues for local businesses to thrive. When it was organized, the chamber covered about 30 square miles of territory, including Milwaukie, Gladstone, Ardenwald, Carver, Clackamas, Barton, Damascus, Boring, Jennings Lodge, Oak Grove, and Wichita. The chamber has offered networking and programs for businesses, which in turn help make North Clackamas economically successful. With North Clackamas County being home to communities with shopping, dining, entertainment, and outdoor recreation, there is plenty of material to promote the region as a great place to live or visit. This 1958 advertisement from the North Clackamas Chamber of Commerce shows the group promoting businesses in Oak Grove. (MM.)

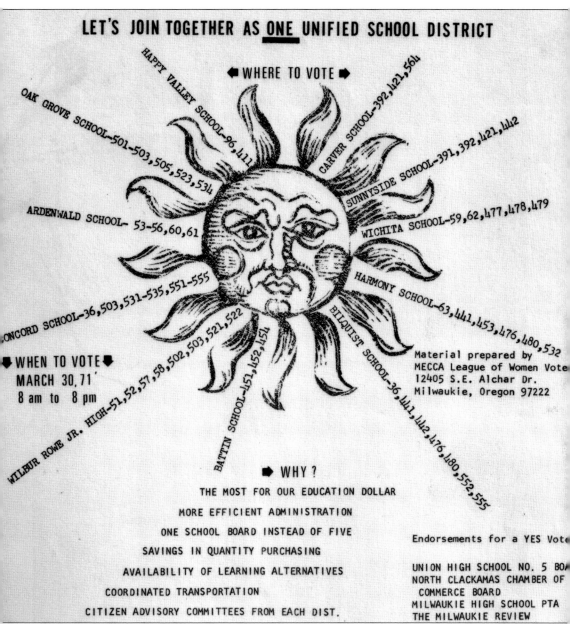

# LET'S JOIN TOGETHER AS <u>ONE</u> UNIFIED SCHOOL DISTRICT

**← WHERE TO VOTE →**

HAPPY VALLEY SCHOOL—96,411

OAK GROVE SCHOOL—501-503,505,523,534

CARVER SCHOOL—392,421,564

SUNNYSIDE SCHOOL—391,392,421,442

ARDENWALD SCHOOL— 53-56,60,61

WICHITA SCHOOL—59,62,477,478,479

CONCORD SCHOOL—36,503,531-535,551-555

HARMONY SCHOOL—63,441,453,476,480,532

BATTIN SCHOOL—451,452,454,457,458,502,503,521,522

WILBUR ROWE JR. HIGH—51,52,57,58,502,503,521,522

BILQUIST SCHOOL—36,441,442,476,480,552,555

**← WHEN TO VOTE →**
MARCH 30, 71'
8 am to 8 pm

Material prepared by
MECCA League of Women Voters
12405 S.E. Alchar Dr.
Milwaukie, Oregon 97222

**→ WHY ?**

THE MOST FOR OUR EDUCATION DOLLAR

MORE EFFICIENT ADMINISTRATION

ONE SCHOOL BOARD INSTEAD OF FIVE

SAVINGS IN QUANTITY PURCHASING

AVAILABILITY OF LEARNING ALTERNATIVES

COORDINATED TRANSPORTATION

CITIZEN ADVISORY COMMITTEES FROM EACH DIST.

Endorsements for a YES Vote

UNION HIGH SCHOOL NO. 5 BOARD
NORTH CLACKAMAS CHAMBER OF
   COMMERCE BOARD
MILWAUKIE HIGH SCHOOL PTA
THE MILWAUKIE REVIEW

When Union High School District No. 5 was formed by a vote of North Clackamas area residents in 1925, it was a step toward the formation of the North Clackamas School District that would occur decades later. Students from the grammar school districts of Milwaukie, Concord, Rock Creek, Harmony, Battin, Clackamas, East Clackamas, Sunnyside, East Mount Scott, Oak Grove, and Wichita could now pursue higher education at the new high school in Milwaukie rather than traveling to Portland or elsewhere. By 1971, North Clackamas residents sought a single unified school district to create more efficient administration and provide a more quality education. Voters approved the creation of the North Clackamas School District, and the adoption of a final plan for this district, also known as administrative school district No. 12, was approved on September 20, 1971. This pamphlet was used to promote the unified school district in 1971. (MM.)

17

The Clackamas Town Center shopping mall opened on March 6, 1981. It cost $125 million to build and became the economic hub of the North Clackamas area. Its unique features included a Clackamas County branch library, a five-screen theater, three towering wood-sculpted cedar trees, community meeting rooms, and an Olympic-sized ice-skating rink. This photograph shows the food court shortly after the mall opened. (CCHS.)

The famous ice rink at Clackamas Town Center provided perfect entertainment for visitors dining in the surrounding food court, and it was later remodeled as the Dorothy Hamill Skating Centre in 1994. It closed in 2003 due to operational expenses and competition from other rinks and was removed. This is how the rink appeared shortly after the mall opened in 1981. (CCHS.)

In 1876, a road going from Harmony to Damascus was established as County Road No. 96. This road became SE Sunnyside Road and is a popular route for traveling across North Clackamas through Clackamas and Happy Valley. This photograph looks west along Sunnyside Road east of 132nd Avenue in 1989, when it was just a two-lane road. (HVHC.)

The North Clackamas Aquatic Park opened on June 9, 1994. The North Clackamas Parks and Recreation District built the swimming complex with three slides, swimming, diving, kids' pools, an outdoor sand volleyball court, and a powerful wave pool that makes visitors feel like they are at the ocean. (NCPRD.)

The North Clackamas Parks and Recreation District was formed in 1990 after getting approval from voters to manage parks and recreation services in the northern part of Clackamas County. The new district took on the maintenance of existing parks in the Milwaukie area and oversaw the construction of the North Clackamas Aquatic Park. This picture from photographer Bill Hupp, who also served as mayor of Milwaukie, shows the ribbon-cutting ceremony for a footbridge at North Clackamas Central Park in 1965. (MM.)

# Two

# FOUNDERS AND SETTLERS

In 1847, Lot Whitcomb, a businessman and politician, journeyed from Illinois to Oregon as part of the Oregon Trail migration. Over the next year, he established a land claim along the Willamette River and founded the town of Milwaukie. He named it after the Wisconsin city, which had varied spelling at the time. Whitcomb later represented Clackamas County in the Oregon Legislature; he died in 1857. (MM.)

Henderson Luelling was an early pioneer who settled in Milwaukie. Henderson's house in Iowa was used for helping slaves escape via the Underground Railroad. In 1847, Luelling brought hundreds of fruit trees to Oregon that would be used to establish the first orchards in the west. He later moved to California and is remembered as the "Father of Pacific Horticulture." (MM.)

Seth Lewelling soon joined his brother Henderson Luelling in becoming a pioneer nurseryman in Milwaukie—each brother adopted a different spelling of their family name. Seth became the sole owner of the family business in 1857. Unlike Henderson, Seth spent the rest of his life in Milwaukie. This photograph shows cherry trees in the Lewelling orchard located near Main Street between Jackson and Monroe Streets in the early 20th century. (CCHS.)

Seth Lewelling developed new fruit varieties, including Black Republican and Bing cherries; the latter was named after his Manchurian foreman Ah Bing. Bing later traveled to China, but due to the Chinese Exclusion Act he was never able to return to Oregon. This photograph of Seth Lewelling features the "spirit image" of Ah Bing—this was a type of photography used at the time. (MM.)

In 1892, Seth Lewelling and his wife, Sophronia, took in a fellow Spiritualist named William S. U'Ren who was suffering a severe asthma attack. U'Ren stayed at the Lewelling home until his health recovered. After their discussions on political reform at Seth's home, U'Ren became a leader in creating the Oregon System of the initiative and referendum. This photograph shows the Lewelling house in 1934. (CCHS.)

In 1848, Joseph Kellogg settled on a land claim next to Lot Whitcomb in the Milwaukie area. With Whitcomb and another neighbor, William Torrence, they laid out a townsite for Milwaukie. Kellogg built a flour mill and sawmill and helped build the *Lot Whitcomb* sidewheeler and other steamboats. (MM.)

A farmer born in Kentucky who later moved to Illinois, Berryman Jennings journeyed to Oregon in a wagon train in 1847. He settled on a donation land claim that would become Jennings Lodge. He helped build the *Lot Whitcomb* sidewheeler in Milwaukie in 1850, served as a receiver at the US Land Office in Oregon City, and was a member of the Oregon Legislature. (CCHS.)

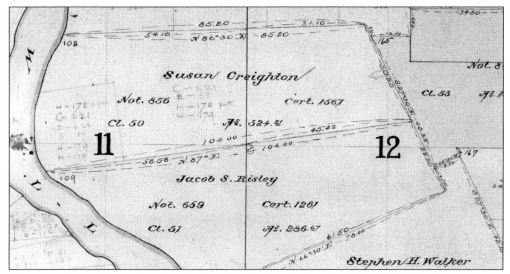

This map shows Susan Creighton's donation land claim in the 1850s. In 1904, the Creighton post office was established to serve Oak Grove. The name was chosen to honor Susan, as postal authorities could not use Oak Grove due to duplication. Born Susan Snyder in 1824 in Ohio, she married Nathaniel Creighton in 1846 in Yamhill, Oregon. After Nathaniel died in 1851, Susan remarried and moved to Washington. (CCHS.)

In 1845, Jacob Swain Risley; his father, Orville; and other family members journeyed from Ohio to Oregon along the Oregon Trail. In 1850, Jacob received a donation land claim just south of Susan Creighton's land claim in Oak Grove. He became a prominent farmer and highly esteemed resident of the county. His son John's wife, Ella, donated the land that became Risley Park. (MM.)

Although the City of Happy Valley did not incorporate until 1965, the settlement of the valley began long before then, when the Deardorff family took hundreds of acreage as donation land claims in 1851. Christian and Matilda Deardorff claimed 640 acres, while their son John (pictured) claimed 320 acres. (HVHC.)

In 1854, John Deardorff married Rachel Ingram. They had three sons—John Bennett, William Albert, and James Henry—and a daughter who died in infancy. John and Rachel were seldom called "Mr. and Mrs. Deardorff." They were more often referred to as "Uncle John" and "Aunt Rachel" within the community. In 1892, a small one-room schoolhouse opened on land the family donated from John Deardorff's land claim. (HVHC)

In 1858, the Deardorff family built the famous Deardorff barn on John's dairy farm, which stood until 1997, when it was torn down to make way for the Happy Valley Heights subdivision. The barn was built in a vernacular style with hewn and mortised timbers fastened together with pegs and the siding attached using square nails. (HVHC)

Edward Pedigo was an Iowa potter who came to North Clackamas in 1854 and settled in a wilderness area possibly for its red clay soil that he could use in his pottery. A community began to form, and a name was needed. Pedigo suggested "Damascus," and it was accepted by the residents in 1866. Pedigo lived in Iowa, Oregon, and Washington when each territory became a state. (WGRL.)

In 1846, Horace Baker and Jane Hattan traveled the Oregon Trail and arrived at the Clackamas River near where the town of Carver would later be platted. Baker (pictured) was a stonemason, so he and Hattan settled on a donation land claim with a basalt rock quarry. Baker supplied stones from his quarry to build several structures in Oregon, including the Willamette Falls Locks. (BCHS.)

Although Jane (Hattan) Baker was not married to Horace before moving to Oregon, they lived together as husband and wife. They came to Oregon with her brother and sister-in-law, Mark and Martha Hattan. Jane and Horace married in 1852 after she was denied half of their 640-acre donation land claim. (BCHS.)

In 1856, Horace Baker had a cabin built with hand-hewn logs and a stone fireplace. Following the deaths of Horace and Jane Baker in 1882 and 1898, respectively, the cabin was inhabited by their descendants for several years. After the home sat vacant for a time, the Old Timers Association of Oregon repaired the structure while maintaining much of the original material. The Baker Cabin, pictured here in 1961, became a historic site and remains one of the oldest log structures in Oregon. The Baker Cabin Historical Society works to preserve the cabin and offers tours. (CCHS.)

In 1914, Stephen Carver was granted permission from Clackamas County to build a railroad from Portland into the locality of Carver, which was then known as Stone. He laid out his plan under the name "Portland and Oregon City Railway Company," but it became known as the Carver Line. Carver hired J. Ralph McIntyre to organize the survey crew. McIntyre began at Harrison and Twenty-Eighth Streets in Milwaukie, and the survey line extended to where Baker's Bridge crossed the Clackamas River. Carver purchased 40 acres from area settler Grant Mumpower and had a home built for himself. He had the acreage surveyed into lots with plans for a town, and the area became known as Carver. Carver died in 1933 in the town named after him. (CCHS.)

In 1852, Francis and Amanda Talbert settled on a donation land claim along 129th Avenue south of King Road in Happy Valley. They arrived one year after the Deardorffs first settled in Happy Valley. The Talbert claim was located to the north of the Mount Talbert butte. In 1873, Francis had a house built at Eighty-Second Avenue and Talbert Road in Clackamas. Francis and Amanda each had children from other marriages and had one surviving son together named John. John Alexander Talbert (pictured) lived on land located southwest of Mount Talbert. John's half-brother Daniel, a son of Francis, owned a homestead on the western slope of Mount Talbert. John became a prominent figure in the area while serving in several public positions. He was a deputy sheriff of Clackamas County from 1879 to 1882 and a county deputy assessor for two years. In 1901, he was elected to serve as the representative for Clackamas in the state legislature. John died in 1929 and was buried in the Clackamas Pioneer Cemetery. (WGRL.)

In 1851, William Tyndall Matlock was elected by Clackamas County to the Oregon Legislature. He was also a land receiver in Oregon City and a county judge. Matlock acquired a 640-acre donation land claim and, in 1852, laid out a plan for a town that would eventually become known as Clackamas. In 1870, a post office was established at Clackamas with Matlock's son Noah as postmaster. (WGRL.)

Born in Montana in 1909, Delbert Johnson established several businesses, including a trucking line, a hog ranch, and a billiard parlor. He became a building contractor in the Milwaukie area and started a mobile home development. Johnson's 45-acre land incorporated as Johnson City in 1970. This photograph shows the city office in the 1970s. Johnson died in 1985. (Kay Mordock.)

# *Three*

# THE WEST SIDE

In 1937, a superhighway connecting Portland to Oregon City was dedicated as McLoughlin Boulevard. The popular route passes through Milwaukie, Oak Grove, and Jennings Lodge near the east bank of the Willamette River in North Clackamas. In 1972, the road became a part of State Highway 99E. This aerial view of McLoughlin Boulevard shows the Fred Meyer at Oak Grove under construction; it opened in 1960. (MM.)

To advance the growth of Milwaukie, town founder Lot Whitcomb hired men to build a steamer to compete with steamboats from Portland. Named the *Lot Whitcomb*, the vessel launched on Christmas Day in 1850 and was the first steam-powered ship built on the Willamette River. The 160-foot-long sidewheeler operated as a passenger and shipping vessel but was later sold to a California company, as its costs were outpacing its profits. (MM.)

During the celebration of the launch of the *Lot Whitcomb* sidewheeler, Capt. Frederick Morse of the schooner *Merchantman* was killed after setting fire to a cannon, which blew up and had its fragments strike him in the neck. His old gravestone, shown here as it appeared in the Milwaukie Pioneer Cemetery in 1961, has been moved to the Milwaukie Museum. (CCHS.)

The year 1850 proved to be a significant time for Milwaukie. The launching of the *Lot Whitcomb* sidewheeler marked the beginning of a shipbuilding industry. Other ships built in Milwaukie included the *Jennie Clark, Senator,* and *Pioneer.* Lot Whitcomb also established a post office with himself as postmaster and launched the *Western Star,* one of the first newspapers in the Oregon Territory. With these successes, Milwaukie competed with Portland and Oregon City to be Oregon's premier city. Portland forged ahead thanks to its own shipbuilding port and ideal location. With Milwaukie no longer in competition with Portland, its population growth slowed into the early 20th century. From 1890 to 1910, Portland's population went from 46,000 to over 200,000. Meanwhile, Milwaukie's population went from under 500 to about 800 during the same time. This photograph shows Main Street in Milwaukie looking west from Jackson Street around 1916. (MM.)

Elk Rock Island was home to the Rock Island Club, a popular dance hall in the early 20th century. The island is located within Clackamas County, but ownership of it was transferred to the City of Portland from private owner Peter Kerr in 1940. This view looks south toward the island in 1912. In the foreground is the Les Harlow boathouse. (CCHS.)

The Rock Island Club remained popular in the Portland area until it was destroyed by a fire in the 1930s. The island is located along the Willamette River near Milwaukie. Sternwheelers were popular forms of river transportation and made the island easily accessible for visitors. The Willamette River was also popular for fishing. This 300-pound sturgeon was caught in the Willamette at Milwaukie in the early 1900s. (CCHS.)

The Standard Mill was built in 1858 by Joseph Kellogg, W.J. Bradbury, and H.W. Eddy. The mill could produce up to 100 barrels of flour per day. It was located near the mouth of Kellogg Creek and the Willamette River by the intersection of McLoughlin Boulevard and Washington Street in Milwaukie. It stood until 1903, when it collapsed. (MM.)

The Milkiewa Feed Mills were established in 1922 by M.S. Shrock. They supplied bulk grain, poultry, dairy, and pigeon feed. They also created fertilizers, spray materials, and other articles necessary for agricultural activities. The name was derived from the Milwaukie Warehouse Company, a business that operated in the same building prior to the opening of the feed mill. The mills closed in 1969. (MM.)

St. John's Episcopal Church was built in 1851 in downtown Milwaukie from materials donated by Milwaukie founder Lot Whitcomb. It was officially consecrated in 1855 by Bishop Thomas Fielding Scott. The original church was relocated to Twenty-First Avenue and Jefferson Street before it was moved by barge along the Willamette River to Sellwood in Portland in 1961 and became known as the Pioneer Church. The building was saved from being scrapped thanks to fundraising efforts by Portland city commissioner Ormond Bean and Southeast Portland Chamber of Commerce committee chairman Dent Thomas. It is one of the oldest churches—possibly *the* oldest—still in use in Oregon. (MM.)

Milwaukie incorporated on February 4, 1903. The first city hall opened in 1908 and was located on Twenty-First Avenue. The city hall on Main Street was dedicated on July 7, 1938, and was constructed by the Public Works Administration. The new building housed council chambers, administrative offices, the fire department, and the city library. This photograph shows the Main Street city hall under construction in 1938. (CCHS.)

Standing 65 feet tall, Milwaukie's famous Pacific dogwood tree was the largest in the country. It was located along Harrison Street near Thirty-Second Avenue. In 1962, the city adopted "Dogwood City of the West" as its official nickname. That same year, the tree suffered extensive damage during the historic Columbus Day Storm and was cut down. The plaque that accompanied the tree was moved to the Milwaukie Museum. (MM.)

After Milwaukie incorporated in 1903, fire protection was desperately needed. A volunteer fire department with horse- and man-drawn hose carts was organized to fight fires. This photograph shows the volunteer fire station on Monroe Street in the 1930s. After the new city hall opened in 1938, the fire department moved there. (MM.)

Although the Milwaukie Band, shown here in the early 1900s, was named after the city, membership was not restricted to Milwaukie. Band members were also from Oak Grove and other neighboring communities. A band hall opened in 1906 at Main and Harrison Streets but later burned to the ground. Admission to see the band perform was 25¢. (MM.)

The Monroe & Roberts blacksmith shop was located on Forty-Second Avenue between Jackson and Monroe Streets in Milwaukie. This is how it appeared in 1914. Owen Roberts also worked as a blacksmith for the Oregon Water Power and Railway Company. In 1903, Roberts served as a member of the first Milwaukie city council. (CCHS.)

This photograph shows the Monroe & Roberts shop interior in 1914. Owen Roberts died in 1905 and was buried in the Milwaukie Pioneer Cemetery. His oldest daughter, Ellen "Nell" Roberts, later became a Milwaukie city recorder and wrote articles for the *Milwaukie Review.* She became well-known for her knowledge of the city and its people. (CCHS.)

On February 16, 1893, the East Side Railway Company's first interurban train, which was an electric railway, arrived in Oregon City from Portland. It was one of the first electric railroads in the United States. The Oregon Water Power and Railway Company incorporated in 1902 and replaced the East Side Railway company as the operator of the interurban lines. The East Side Railway Company built the carbarn shops in Milwaukie, and these photographs show the crew and the interior of the repair shop after it was taken over by the Oregon Water Power and Railway Company in the early 1900s. A carbarn is a building used for the housing and maintenance of railway cars. (Both, CCHS.)

George Wissinger was born in Wisconsin in 1870. He later moved to Oregon to join his brother Oscar, and together they partnered in a general merchandise business in Milwaukie. It was the only store of its kind in the area and served people from Ardenwald, Wichita, Oak Grove, and other communities. This is how the Wissingers' store appeared in 1894. (CCHS.)

The Milwaukie streetcar depot was located on the corner of Front (later McLoughlin Boulevard) and Monroe Streets and was used by Milwaukie-area residents to ride by rail to Portland and Oregon City. This photograph shows the Portland Railway Light and Power Company ticket office at the station around 1913. (MM.)

This undated (likely early 1900s) photograph shows the Ullrich Saloon in Milwaukie. Mr. Ullrich is standing at far right. The man sitting in the chair is Noah Hubler. Hubler was born in Ohio in 1832 and moved to Oregon in the 1850s. For a time, he worked as a foreman in Seth Lewelling's orchard and also operated a tavern in Milwaukie. Hubler took pride in being Milwaukie's first police officer, an honor he bestowed upon himself because he owned a gun and a badge. The man in the background (behind the bar) is Jesse Keck. In 1903, Keck was appointed Milwaukie's first town marshal. He was responsible for enforcing town ordinances and keeping the peace. (MM.)

Crystal Lake Park began on the property of Otto Witte. When Witte discovered springs on his property, he had a pond built. He placed trout in the pond and invited friends over to go fishing. After he started charging admission to outsiders to fish, Witte established the Crystal Lake Amusement Park. This photograph shows the Crystal Lake pool in 1910. (MM.)

Crystal Lake Park opened on May 1, 1908. The park occupied 18 acres on the north side of Harrison Street in Milwaukie. The property featured a baseball ground, dance hall, picnic area, and bowling alley. The name came from the crystal-clear water in the pond. Here, a game of tug of war is being played at the park in the 1920s. (CCHS.)

Following the incorporation of Milwaukie in 1903, the city enacted several ordinances, such as the regulation of storage of gunpowder, dynamite, and other explosives; improving streets; prohibiting riding bicycles on sidewalks; and the regulation of roaming livestock on the streets. This photograph shows Twenty-First Avenue in Milwaukie in the early 1920s. (MM.)

By the end of World War II, Milwaukie's population was about 5,000. Wartime housing projects and postwar residential developments in the area contributed to a dramatic rise in the city's population. By 1970, the city's population had tripled to over 16,000. This photograph shows Milwaukie at Main and Washington Streets in the late 1960s. (MM.)

46

The flood of 1890 left behind destruction at the Harlow residence in Milwaukie, as shown here. In early February 1890, snowmelt and heavy rain caused the Willamette and Clackamas Rivers to rapidly rise and flood the area. Major flood events have occurred along the Willamette River in 1861, 1890, 1923, 1964, and 1996. (CCHS.)

In December 1964, Arctic cold temperatures swept into Oregon and brought 11 inches of snow to the valley floor. A Pineapple Express warm front caused freezing temperatures to rise into the upper 50s in just two days, and with additional heavy rain, another flooding disaster came to communities along the Willamette River. Here, a boat passes by the Pendleton Woolen Mills in Milwaukie during the flood of 1964. (CCHS.)

Philip Henneman was born in 1840 in Germany and immigrated to the United States in the 1860s. His wife, Elizabeth, immigrated from Germany in 1870, and they were married that year. The Hennemans came to Milwaukie around 1882, and the family started one of the region's first commercial berry farms on 11 acres between Washington Street and Lake Road. This photograph shows the Henneman strawberry fields in Milwaukie. (MM.)

Schei (or Sahei) Watanabe was born in Japan in 1869. He came to the United States in 1901 and lived in California before moving to Milwaukie and establishing a celery farm near Railroad Avenue. During World War II, he was placed in an internment camp, and a neighbor managed the farm shown in this photograph. Watanabe died in 1945. (MM.)

When William and Mary Perry came to Milwaukie, they purchased a small drugstore on Main Street. Perry's Pharmacy consistently grew over the years until it moved into a new building on Main Street at Monroe Street. The soda fountain inside the store was a popular meeting place for many people who came for coffee, a milkshake, or Green River sodas. This is how the pharmacy appeared in 1957. (MM.)

In 1909, a young Ralph Cooper started working at W.S. Lehman's meat market on Main Street in Milwaukie. At that time, the market's owner went to places like Sunnyside and Clackamas to sell meat off a horse-drawn wagon. Cooper purchased the market in 1919, and it became known as the Ralph Cooper Meat Market. This is how the market appeared in 1950. (MM.)

In 1947, Milwaukie had a centennial celebration to commemorate the arrival of pioneer horticulturist Henderson Luelling. In 1950, Milwaukie celebrated the Founders Centennial to honor Lot Whitcomb, Joseph Kellogg, Seth Lewelling, and other city founders. This photograph shows the parade that traveled down Main Street during the Founders Centennial. (MM.)

In 1954, Milwaukie High School's boys' basketball team won the state championship by defeating the Eugene Axemen 52–44. The Mustangs were greeted with a rally in Milwaukie celebrating their title before an estimated crowd of 3,000 people. Mayor Leonard Mullan and school superintendent Owen Sabin celebrated the team at the rally shown here. (MM.)

In 1889, Alfred Luelling started a circulating library in Milwaukie in the offices of a local attorney. The library moved to several locations over the years, including the old city hall and Perry's Pharmacy. In 1961, longtime library advocate Florence (Olson) Ledding left her home to the city for the purpose of turning it into a library. This photograph shows the Ledding Library in the 1960s. (MM.)

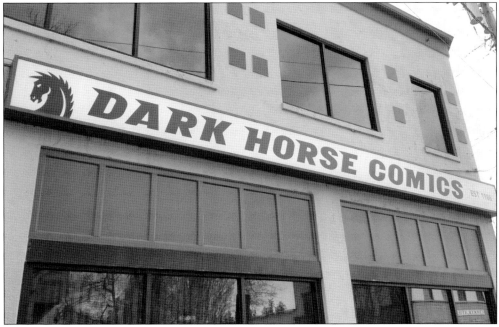

Dark Horse Comics was founded in Milwaukie by Mike Richardson in 1986. Dark Horse became the third-largest comics publisher in the United States behind DC and Marvel. Among the titles Dark Horse has published include *Hellboy*, *The Mask*, Frank Miller's *Sin City*, *Buffy the Vampire Slayer*, and *Star Wars*. (MM.)

The P&C Tools Manufacturing Company was established in 1923 in Milwaukie and was noted for its well-made socket wrenches, ratchets, and screwdrivers. It became the Stanley-Proto Industrial Tools Plant in 1984 and closed in 1990. (MM.)

Milwaukie landmark Bernard's Garage was started by Joe Bernard Sr. in 1925 at the corner of Twenty-Fifth Avenue and Washington Street. The family has a rich legacy of community service. Joe Bernard's son and grandson each served as mayor of Milwaukie. The iconic "B" sign from the garage is now on display at the Milwaukie Museum. (MM.)

This photograph, taken from the top of Thiessen Hill along Thiessen Road in unincorporated North Clackamas in the early 1940s, shows what the area looked like before the housing boom that followed World War II. The farmlands that once occupied the countryside transformed into residential developments that would continue for decades to come and foretold a similar fate for many communities in the North Clackamas region. In Milwaukie, the Kellogg Park housing development of 600 units contributed to the postwar housing boom, and many industries and commercial businesses opened along McLoughlin Boulevard. Soon, the North Clackamas Chamber of Commerce would organize as a nonprofit and bring together business interests in the region. (MM).

Art Lacey's Bomber Station, located along McLoughlin Boulevard (Highway 99E) in Oak Grove, was dedicated on July 27, 1947. Lacey was a former pilot and worked for the US Army Corps of Engineers during World War II. He paid $15,000 to purchase the B-17 bomber in Oklahoma and flew it to Oregon to be set atop his service station. (CCHS.)

The Bomber Station in Oak Grove became a regional landmark and a famous roadside attraction. In 1948, Arthur "Art" Lacey opened a restaurant at his service station. Lacey kept a guest register at the Bomber Station, and it contained names of visitors from all over the world. Lacey died in 2000. The bomber plane was removed for restoration in 2014. (CCHS.)

Typhoon Freda struck the Pacific Northwest on October 12, 1962, and unleashed wind gusts of over 100 miles per hour across Oregon. The devastating storm became known as the Columbus Day Storm and was nicknamed the "Big Blow." These photographs show damage to the Fred Meyer in Oak Grove. The destruction caused by the Columbus Day Storm included toppling trees and power lines, reducing barns to scrap wood, and widespread damage to thousands of homes and buildings. The storm was considered to be the greatest natural disaster on the West Coast since the 1906 San Francisco earthquake. (Both, CCHS.)

This photograph shows Oak Grove and looks west on Oak Grove Boulevard from Rupert Drive in 1909. Resident Harvey G. Starkweather said that the name for the community was suggested by Edward W. Cornell, a member of the surveying party that platted the area in the 1890s. Cornell's suggestion came from the crew eating lunch in a grove of oak trees in the northwestern part of the tract. (CCHS.)

This view shows Oak Grove at Oatfield and Courtney Roads in 1890. Oatfield Road was named after the Oatfield family. Michael Oatfield came to Oregon in the 1860s and purchased the Orrin Kellogg donation land claim, which was to the east of the Susan Creighton claim. Oatfield operated an orchard and farm across 600 acres. He married Minerva Thessing, and they became a beloved pioneer family. (CCHS.)

The Oak Grove Diner opened in the 1930s with Anne E. Edwards as its owner. The diner was inside a repurposed electric railroad car and located along McLoughlin and Oak Grove Boulevards in Oak Grove. In the 1960s, it moved to Banks, Oregon, and later got scrapped. (CCHS.)

In the 1890s, an interurban electric railway was constructed between Portland and Oregon City and passed through Milwaukie, Oak Grove, and Jennings Lodge. This photograph shows an interurban car at Jennings Crossing with McLoughlin Boulevard in 1956. New electric rail lines came to North Clackamas (with the MAX Light Rail to Clackamas Town Center) in 2012 and Milwaukie in 2015. (CCHS.)

This photograph shows the *Young America* at the German Methodists' boat landing near Oak Grove in 1890. Steamboats would make stops at Oak Grove Beach and Cedar Grove Park, by Jennings Lodge, to drop off and pick up people from picnics and dances. (CCHS.)

This undated photograph shows Oak Grove Beach, located along the Willamette River at the foot of Central Avenue (now Oak Grove Boulevard) in Oak Grove. This was a popular location for swimming, picnicking, dancing, and boating, and it even had cottages available for rent. (MM.)

The Oak Lodge Fire Department responded to the Milwaukie High School gym fire in 1963. The fire department is one example of a service or organization that was the result of collaboration between the communities of Oak Grove and Jennings Lodge. Other examples include Oak Lodge Water Services District, Oak Lodge Library, and Oak Lodge History Detectives. The name "Oak Lodge" has also been used to refer to the area as a whole. (MM.)

This photograph shows the Jennings Lodge station and welcome arch in 1916. Settler Berryman Jennings served as the first Grand Master of the Masonic Grand Lodge AF & AM of Oregon. After his death in 1888, half of his donation land claim was given to his daughter Addie, who—with her husband, Frank—platted Jennings Lodge in 1903. (CCHS.)

The Jennings post office was established on November 3, 1910, with Lenora Miller as postmaster. The name of the office was changed to Jennings Lodge in 1911. The name possibly originated because Berryman Jennings helped form a Masonic lodge in Sacramento, California, named Berryman Lodge, which later changed its name to Jennings Lodge. This could be why Jennings Lodge was chosen as the name of the community. This photograph shows the Blue Front Grocery in Jennings Lodge as it appeared in 1917. The store was opened in 1912 by H.J. Batdorf and was located along the trolley line on Hull Avenue just east of McLoughlin Boulevard. (CCHS.)

Grace Community Congregational Church on SE Blanton Street in Jennings Lodge was organized by Rev. H.N. Smith after he saw a need for religious education among the community's children. When the building became too small to accommodate its congregation, the church underwent an extreme makeover when it was razed and enlarged in 1922. This photograph shows the church celebrating its first Easter in 1915. (CCHS.)

Edward E. Roethe was born in 1870 in Iowa. He moved to the Jennings Lodge area with his parents in 1889 and lived on property located where Roethe Road is today. Produce from the Roethe farm was sent to markets from Roethe's Landing along the Willamette River, which is shown here around 1905 with Edward Roethe at left. (CCHS.)

This 1905 photograph shows members of the Oatfield family at Risley's Landing along the Willamette River as they wait for a steamboat to take their crop of potatoes to Portland. Pictured are brothers John and Philip Oatfield (sons of Michael and Minerva Oatfield) with Philip's daughter Inez sitting on John's lap. The photograph was taken by Ella Risley, wife of John Risley. (MM.)

This 1941 photograph was taken at Oatfield Hill at what is now the intersection of Oatfield and Robin Roads. The Oatfield brothers, Philip and John, were farmers in this area. The hillside was also platted as Concord Crest by Elsie Oatfield, John's widow. The car belonged to Paul Laudien, husband of Phil Oatfield's daughter Irene Oatfield; Laudien is the person who took this photograph. (MM.)

The Philip Oatfield home is shown here just after completion in 1903. Philip is standing in front of the house. He was one of the children of Michael and Minerva Oatfield, the pioneer family for whom Oatfield Road was named. The census-designated place of Oatfield in unincorporated North Clackamas received its name from the road. The house was located on the east side of Oatfield Road near Risley Avenue. The Oatfield home stood as a historic landmark for more than a century. The house survived when farmlands in the area were developed into suburban neighborhoods. However, it was demolished in 2017 after it fell into disrepair. (MM.)

Johnson City was incorporated on June 16, 1970. At the time, the city was unique, as it was entirely owned by Delbert Johnson. Johnson unsuccessfully tried to annex his land of manufactured homes, shown here in the 1970s, to Gladstone. In 1968, the residents attempted to incorporate but were vetoed by county commissioners. In 1970, the Oregon Supreme Court allowed a vote by the residents to incorporate. (Kay Mordock.)

Johnson City is like other cities in that it has a mayor, city council, city park, and municipal services, but it stands out as the only incorporated city of manufactured homes in the United States. Johnson City's lake, shown here in the 1970s, was named by founder Delbert Johnson in honor of his wife, Leona. (Kay Mordock.)

## Four

# THE EAST SIDE

The Clackamas community, located on the eastern side of Highway 213 and Interstate 205, was also known as Marshfield due to a filed plat map and an Oregon & California Railroad station that had that name in 1870. In December 1870, the Clackamas post office was established, and the station later changed its name. This photograph shows farmland at Clackamas near Mather Road in 1907. (CCHS.)

The post office, store, and residence of Arthur Mather, located at Ninety-Fourth Avenue and Clackamas Road, is shown here in 1891. Mather's post office and store were considered the central hub of the Clackamas community. The home next to the store was replaced with a new one sometime in the 1890s. After Mather died, he was remembered as one of the most prominent residents of Clackamas County. (CCHS.)

This 1918 photograph in Clackamas shows Arthur Mather's store and post office at left. The building also served as the railroad agency for the Oregon & California Railroad, which was succeeded by Southern Pacific. For 60 years, the post office was operated by the Mather family, with Arthur's daughter Ethel following in his footsteps as postmaster. The Mather residence next to the store was later relocated to Sunnyside Commons at Sunnyside Road and 132nd Avenue. (CCHS.)

This Clackamas street scene from 1915 shows the Haberlach store at left at the corner of Clackamas Road and Eighty-Second Drive. The Haberlach family also operated a feed and flour mill. On Saturday nights, the upstairs level of the mill was used as a community dance hall. As the Clackamas population grew, the need came for a larger grocery and merchandise establishment. Fred Meyer acquired 14 acres in the 1960s for a new store along Eighty-Second Drive, and the store opened in 1979. When the community needed fire protection, the Clackamas Fire Station began with about 20 volunteers in a garage east of the Clackamas Grade School. The fire station opened in 1961; an addition was put on in 1970 to make room for firefighters to sleep. Clackamas changed significantly with the openings of many businesses along Eighty-second Drive and an industrial boom by Highway 212, which led to the Arthur Mather place no longer being the center of the community. (CCHS.)

The army camp at Clackamas began as the Clackamas Rifle Range when it opened for its first season in 1909. The purpose of the range was to train men to use the Springfield rifle. The rifle range was renamed Camp Benson after Frank Benson (governor of Oregon from 1909 to 1910), and the Oregon National Guard began training there. The trainees slept in tents until barracks were built after World War I. During World War I, almost 1,500 men were stationed at the camp. The camp was renamed again to Camp Withycombe after James Withycombe (governor of Oregon from 1915 to 1919). Clackamas residents would walk to the railroad station to watch the troops depart from the camp. This 1918 photograph shows some of the tents used by soldiers at the camp. (CCHS.)

Camp Withycombe is pictured here in 1916. The Clackamas site served as a mobilization camp during the 1916 Mexican border campaign, World War I, and World War II. Camp Withycombe became the main depot for all the tanks, artillery, and military equipment in the state. The site later became home to the Oregon Military Museum. (CCHS.)

A crowd watches as US Army troops from Camp Withycombe march down a street in Clackamas in 1916. The troops were headed to the Mexican border during the Mexican Revolution. Later, similar scenes would play out as troops marched off to serve during World War I. (CCHS.)

This 1907 photograph shows the Haberlach store at Clackamas Road and Eighty-Second Drive in Clackamas. Next door to the store was the Haberlach home that was built in the 1890s for Gustav and Auguste Haberlach. The man on the wagon is Billy Danforth, who was known to the Haberlachs as "Uncle Billy" for delivering groceries from the store. (CCHS.)

Sam Roake, shown here in 1910, was a Rural Free Delivery (RFD) mail carrier in Clackamas. After being established in the late 19th century, RFD became a blessing for those living in the North Clackamas region, as they no longer had to travel long distances to get their mail. (CCHS.)

Sam Roake, shown here on Eighty-Second Drive in Clackamas in 1910, lived along Clackamas Road. He would gather sword ferns by the bundle and sell them to florists in Portland, delivering them in boxes using this wagon. Strawberries from fields in Clackamas were also gathered by locals and sold in Portland. (CCHS.)

The Herrington family owned the Clackamas Hotel, shown here in 1895. The hotel was located across the road from the Mather store and a short walk away from the railroad depot. Much like the Clackamas Hotel, people in the area have come and gone, and massive changes have occurred across much of the North Clackamas region. (CCHS.)

The Clackamas Congregational Church, shown here in 1907, was organized in 1895. It was first located along Clackamas Road, then Church Street, and finally moved to Webster Road in Milwaukie in the 1960s and became the Clackamas United Church of Christ. The Methodist church in Clackamas was built in 1881 at the corner of Eighty-Second Drive and Church Street; the first building burned down, and a second one was built later. (CCHS.)

In the early 1900s, the Frank Ott family began operating a mill and the Sunnyside Country Store along Sunnyside Road. For decades, the store was the commerce center for the Sunnyside community, a former census-designated place. Locals went there to buy everything from nails to baking flour to livestock feed. This photograph is from the 1950s. (CCHS.)

Around 1946, a giant tree fell across Sieben Creek and created a spontaneous dam on the Hubbard property south of Sunnyside Road. The new pond gave Wally Hubbard the idea to turn the impeded creek into a swimming hole. The Army veteran later had a concrete dam built and added amenities, and Wally's Dam became a popular destination for thousands of locals. (HVHC.)

Much like the Deardorff family, after non-Indigenous people reached Happy Valley, they began to farm. Several springs and fertile soil made it an ideal location for those looking to establish farms. As more and more people moved in and claimed valley acreage, a settlement of farmers was established, and it soon became a peaceful community of neighbors. Happy Valley is pictured here in a 1915 view looking west toward Mount Scott. (HVHC.)

In 1888, the Strickrott family settled in Happy Valley. After first living in a log cabin, they built a house on Mount Scott Boulevard. Many different crops were grown in Happy Valley. Grain was used to make bread and also to produce hay for feeding cows and horses. This photograph shows Mr. Strickrott and his horse team at work on their farm. (CCHS.)

Common vegetables grown in Happy Valley included beans, peas, potatoes, corn, and cabbage. The valley's plentiful fruit trees produced pears, apples, plums, and cherries. Some of the berries cultivated in the area included strawberries, boysenberries, blackberries, and raspberries. This photograph shows the barn on the Strickrott family farm. (CCHS.)

The Zinsers became a prominent family in Happy Valley. In 1890, John George Zinser bought land along King Road and built a house on the spot that would become the city hall and, later, the policing station. John's brother Charles Frederick built a log cabin at the corner of Mount Scott Boulevard and Ridgecrest Road. This image shows the Charles Frederick Zinser home before it became a shop and grainery. (HVHC.)

Happy Valley's earliest roads were just trails made by wagons. Roads were muddy in the winter and dusty in summer. It was impossible to go down or up a steep road during a rainy season. To build roads, people blasted stumps with dynamite and used horse-drawn slip scrapers and shovels. Here, Happy Valley road work is being done in 1915. (CCHS.)

Happy Valley has had many names in the course of its history. It was first referred to as the Deardorff Settlement and the Deardorff Valley after the first non-Indigenous family in the area. The name Happy Hollow emerged from a story of community boys getting happily drunk from apple cider. East Mount Scott came from the school's name for a time during the first half of the 20th century. Christilla Valley arose from a meeting held at the valley's school in 1902—this name was a combination of Christian (Chris) and Matilda (Tilla) Deardorff as a tribute to them. Despite all these different names for the same geographic area, only one has been used by realtors in advertisements for selling acreage. For this reason, Happy Valley is believed to have been popularized by realtors either as a combination of the city's other names or as an optimistic strategy used to sell property. This photograph shows the city limits along 122nd Avenue in 1988. (HVHC.)

The Happy Valley Evangelical Church began in 1891, and the first building consisted of just one room. Before the church was built, the congregants went to Sunnyside or Rock Creek for worship. The original building was torn down in 1915 and replaced with a larger one seen here in 1937. The church is located along 129th Avenue. (HVHC.)

Across the street from the Happy Valley Evangelical Church is the Happy Valley Fire Station, shown here in 1987. Happy Valley Rural Fire District No. 65 was formed by volunteers in 1949. In 1956, the fire department began sponsoring a July 4th fireworks show that became the most popular event of the year in the city. The fire station was built in the 1950s. (HVHC.)

In 1901, Charles Rebstock purchased the house built by John George Zinser along King Road. This house was the birthplace of Charles's son, Edward. Edward became affectionately known as "Mr. Happy Valley" due to his generosity. The City of Happy Valley purchased the house to renovate it for use as a city hall, but due to termite damage, it was torn down, and a new city hall building was erected instead. (HVHC.)

In 1965, Happy Valley faced the possibility that the peaceful, nature-blessed, and isolated community could be swallowed up by annexation into the commercialism of—and paying taxes to—the City of Portland. When Portland annexed the Willamette National Cemetery, Happy Valley residents came together to discuss the option of incorporation. This 1992 photograph by Bud Unruh looks toward Scouters Mountain from Mount Scott. (HVHC.)

On August 25, 1965, Happy Valley residents held a special election to decide whether to incorporate. Votes were cast at the fire station, and the results favored incorporation 111-66. The city council held its first meeting on November 17, 1965, at the fire station; city council meetings were then held at the water district office across the street until the city hall, shown here in 1994, was built. (HVHC.)

It might be hard to believe that Happy Valley was once a small, isolated community of farmers with horse pastures. Luckily, local resident Bud Unruh photographed scenes like this pasture in 1989 to show what the city was once like. This field was across the road from where Happy Valley Elementary and Middle Schools are now located. (HVHC.)

William Monner built a sawmill (shown here in 1925) with his brother-in-law at 162nd Avenue in Happy Valley. Much of the logging Monner did in the area was from 147th Avenue down the hill to Hagen Road. He used a team of horses to haul logs to the mill, which employed about six or seven people. Clackamas County named Monner Road after him. (CCHS.)

The Deardorff Barn (in the foreground) and the Happy Valley Elementary School appear in this photograph looking northwest over Happy Valley in 1988. This was before Happy Valley's population boom that began in the 1990s and led to it becoming one of the fastest-growing cities in Oregon in terms of percentage increase. The school, barn, and pasture have since been replaced by new schools and a residential development. (HVHC.)

The big barn in this 1989 picture taken by photographer Bud Unruh was located along Sunnyside Road east of 132nd Avenue. It was built sometime in the early 20th century by Ed Ott after he bought the property from his father, Florian. Ed was the half-brother of Frank Ott, owner of the Sunnyside Country Store and mill. The Ott barn stood for almost a century in an area where locals tended filbert orchards in the 1900s. The structure was one of the last remaining historic barns in the Happy Valley area but was removed in 2005 to make way for the widening of Sunnyside Road to relieve congestion on what was becoming a very busy commuter route through Clackamas and Happy Valley. (HVHC.)

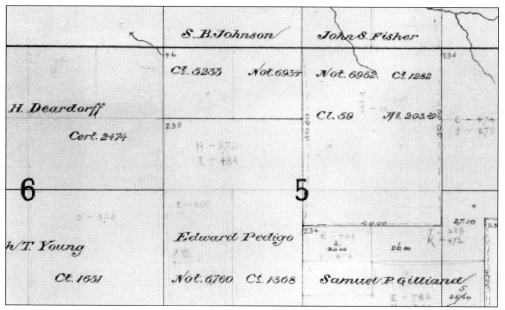

The Damascus post office was established on August 26, 1867, with John Smith Fisher—who took a donation land claim there in the early 1850s—as postmaster. This map shows the location of Fisher's land claim, which stretched from Foster Road north to Rock Creek. Fisher was the son-in-law of Edward Pedigo, the potter from Iowa who is credited with naming Damascus. (CCHS.)

The Damascus Pioneer Cemetery, located at SE Chitwood Road, is the resting place of some of the early non-Indigenous residents of the Damascus area. Land for the Damascus Cemetery was donated by James and Margaret Chitwood. Other pioneer cemeteries in North Clackamas include Milwaukie, Clackamas, Sunnyside, and Deardorff (also known as Christilla). (WGRL.)

In the 1800s, Damascus residents received their mail once a week, when Ed Pedigo rode his horse to Milwaukie. It was normal for people to get mail for their neighbors. The establishment of churches provided the community with places of fellowship for neighbors to come together. One such place was the aptly named Damascus Community Church, which is shown in this 1951 Bible school photograph. (Trena Heydel.)

In 1959, Damascus hosted one of the largest Oregon Centennial celebrations, with tens of thousands of people attending, and the Damascus Centennial Park was created. Damascus received a flood of publicity for the celebration, as did the city's Little World's Fair in 1962. This photograph shows the Centennial Peace Candle in Damascus in 1959. (CCHS.)

The original Centennial Peace Candle, shown in this 1959 image, was made from chicken wire, cut-up oil drums, and 20 tons of wax. It burned for 100 days in honor of Oregon's statehood centennial. A concrete replica was cast in 1962 during the Damascus Little World's Fair celebration, which was held the same year as the World's Fair in Seattle. In 2009, the Centennial Peace Candle was relit in honor of the Oregon Sesquicentennial. In 1973, just to the west of Damascus Centennial Park, the Damascus Square Shopping Center opened with Thriftway as the first supermarket in town. Damascus had its own water district until 2000, when it merged with the Mount Scott Water District to form the Sunrise Water District. Also in 2000, Damascus had a population over 9,000 and was on its way toward municipal incorporation. (CCHS.)

The Damascus Trading Post was one of the buildings used during the Little World's Fair in 1962 to celebrate the town's frontier days. Damascus received notable publicity during the 1959 and 1962 celebrations and also during the area's time as an incorporated city. Damascus became a municipality in 2004, and Dee Wescott, owner of Wescott's Auto Re-Styling, was elected as the city's first mayor. (CCHS.)

Forty-two years after Damascus celebrated its past with the Little World's Fair, residents looked to the future and elected to incorporate. The 2004 election also incorporated the nearby community of Carver into the City of Damascus. The city hall opened in Damascus Square. After the city was unable to pass a comprehensive plan or provide basic services, Damascus residents approved disincorporation in 2016. (CCHS.)

In 1877, a fish hatchery opened on the Clackamas River in present-day Carver near Clear Creek. The hatchery was constructed on a tract of land from Horace and Jane Baker's donation land claim. The hatchery was abandoned in the early 1880s but later reopened by the State of Oregon and operated by the federal government. In the early 1900s, the hatchery was moved downriver to a site near the community of Clackamas. Carver was previously known as Stone—named for Dr. Livingston Stone, a pioneer in American fish culture. Dr. Stone was a deputy fish commissioner and a superintendent of the Clackamas River hatchery, which is believed to be the second federal fish hatchery in the United States. This photograph shows fish jetties for the hatchery at Carver in 1880. (CCHS.)

When the Stone post office opened at the hatchery in 1896, the area was also given the Stone name. After this office was discontinued, the Carver post office was established near Baker's Bridge along the Clackamas River; it closed in the late 1930s. This photograph looks west and shows the town of Carver in 1920. (CCHS.)

The Logan German Methodist Church, pictured in 1983, was built in 1895 and abandoned in the 1920s in Logan, a small unincorporated town southeast of Carver. It was purchased in 1967 by the Old Timer's Association and moved to the Baker Cabin site. The Baker Cabin Historical Society hosts weddings at the site. (CCHS.)

Horace Baker established a ferry across the Clackamas River in 1872 near the mouth of Clear Creek. It remained in use until a bridge (shown here in 1910) was built in 1883. The bridge was built one year after Horace's death and was given the name Baker's Bridge. It remained in use until a new bridge replaced it in 1930. (CCHS.)

With more people moving into Clackamas County and roads still unpaved, a quicker mode of transportation was needed—something faster than horse-drawn wagons. Stephen Carver laid out his plan for a railroad that would pass through Stone, as it was then known. The "galloping goose" railcar shown here was used by residents of Carver for trips along the Portland and Oregon City Railroad. (CCHS.)

Baker's Ferry, shown here in 1881, was one of the names used to refer to the area that eventually became Carver. An earlier name was Baker's Quarry, after stonemason Horace Baker's nearby rock quarry. In 1883, after a bridge was built to replace the ferry, the area was known as Baker's Bridge. The next name was Stone, after hatchery superintendent Livingston Stone, and finally Carver, for Stephen Carver. (CCHS.)

The famous old covered Baker's Bridge was replaced with a new bridge built in 1930. This photograph shows the new bridge in 1934. Near the bridge, L.V. and "Dolly" Mumpower ran a park along the Clackamas River where the Mumpower sawmill stood for years. (CCHS.)

In 1901, W.P. Kirchem, Fred Riebhoff, John J. Hattan, F.D. Mumpower, and J.W. Watts filed articles of incorporation for a creamery at Carver, then known as Stone. About 100 milk cows were available at Stone, which made a creamery there a profitable business opportunity. It was called the Clear Creek Creamery, and this is how it appeared in 1908. (CCHS.)

This 1908 photograph shows the interior of the Clear Creek Creamery. It was located on the south side of the Clackamas River. The creamery closed in 1936, and the building was removed in 1952. (CCHS.)

The Mumpower sawmill in Carver is shown here in 1910 with Baker's Bridge in the background. Pictured here are (left to right) Joseph Mumpower, Paul Mumpower, Olin Skirvin, Verle Mumpower, Audrey Skirvin, William Mumpower, and Joseph Grant Mumpower. (CCHS.)

The Echo Inn lunch room in Carver was established in 1922 by Paul and Echo Mumpower. Paul was a grandson of Joseph and Julia Mumpower, who moved to the area in the 1880s and became one of the most prominent families in the community. This photograph shows the Echo Inn in 1923. (CCHS.)

The community of Barton was named after Barton, Wisconsin, by Ernest Burghardt, who had previously lived near there. He came to Oregon in 1876 with his wife, Emelia, and settled along Deep Creek, where he started a gristmill (shown in this 1880s photograph) and a sawmill. He opened a store and then established the Barton post office on May 16, 1896. (CCHS.)

This photograph shows the Barton post office at H.F. Gibson's store in the 1910s. Ernest Burghardt, along with Gibson and others, filed a Barton plat map with Clackamas County in 1904 to formally establish a community. Located near Barton is Barton Park, which is a popular destination in the region. The park provides camping, picnicking, and a boat ramp with a great swimming spot in the Clackamas River. (CCHS.)

# *Five*

# OUR SCHOOLS

In 1892, the first school in Happy Valley was built on an acre of land donated by John Bennett Deardorff. One teacher taught all grades—from one through eight—in one room. The first school was called Christilla School, a name used to honor Chris and Tilla Deardorff, the first non-Indigenous settlers in Happy Valley. This photograph shows a playground scene at the Christilla School in 1912. (CCHS.)

The first Happy Valley school was replaced by a larger one in 1917, with additional classrooms added to it over the years. In 1960, a large brick building was constructed at Happy Valley Elementary School, with a north section added in 1967. In 2008, the old Happy Valley Elementary School (shown here with the bell from the original schoolhouse in the 1970s) was torn down, and new elementary and middle school buildings were constructed. In addition to these new schools, several other schools were built in the early 21st century to keep pace with Happy Valley's booming population. Among these schools are Spring Mountain Elementary (built in 2000), Scouters Mountain and Verne A. Duncan Elementary (built in 2009), and Rock Creek Middle School (built in 2010), which was later renovated and converted into Adrienne C. Nelson High School—the first high school located within Happy Valley city limits. (HVHC.)

In 1884, the Sunnyside School (shown in this 1927 photograph) was established at the northeast corner of 122nd Avenue and Sunnyside Road. As attendance began outgrowing and crowding this school building, the school board chose a property along Hubbard Lane (later renamed 132nd Avenue) for a new school, and Sunnyside Elementary School was dedicated on November 10, 1949. (HVHC.)

George Deardorff donated the land for the Rock Creek School in 1895. The school, pictured here in 1909, was located at the corner of 172nd Avenue and Sunnyside Road. After the Rock Creek School District merged with the Clackamas School District, the school remained empty until a church group rented it. (WGRL.)

Children at the Union School (pictured) in Damascus carried water to the school from a spring located about a quarter mile away. They took turns drinking from a dipper or would pass water from desk to desk. The Union School District was established in 1886, while the Damascus "Pioneer" School was founded in 1877. The Damascus-Union District later consolidated with the Gresham-Barlow School District in 1994. (WGRL.)

The first Hillsview School was built around 1880 and located north of the Damascus Union School near Clackamas County's border with Multnomah County. A second school, shown in this photograph, was built in the early 1900s across the road from the first one. Hillsview School closed in 1948. (WGRL.)

Public school in the Carver area began in the late 1800s with the Hatchery School, named after the nearby Clackamas River fish hatchery. A school built in the early 1900s is pictured here in 1934. The next Carver Grade School was built in 1936 and merged with the Clackamas School District in 1955. (CCHS.)

This photograph shows all of the students at the Carver Grade School in 1923. After the Carver School District consolidated with the Clackamas School District in 1955, only kindergarten through second grade students continued to go to school in Carver, while the others were bused to Clackamas. Carver students attended Verne Duncan Elementary after it opened in 2009. (CCHS.)

The Clackamas School District had a school near the Clackamas River called the East Clackamas School, which was located south of what is now Highway 212 and later consolidated with Clackamas Elementary. To the west, students attended the Clackamas School, which is shown here in 1890. (CCHS.)

Clackamas children first went to school at the Baptist church. After the church burned down, a small two-room school was built in 1882; it is located on the right in this 1910 photograph. On the left is the two-story Clackamas School that succeeded the smaller building. After the two-story Clackamas School building was constructed, the smaller school was torn down. (CCHS.)

The Parent-Teachers Association (PTA) was organized at the Clackamas School in 1924. Among the group's goals was raising money to purchase encyclopedias for the classrooms, acquire school buses, and maintain the school building. Toilets were installed inside the school in 1929, and hot lunches were first served in 1938. This photograph shows the Clackamas School interior in 1918. (MM.)

In the center of the Clackamas School was a bell tower. When the bell rang, the students lined up before marching into the school. In 1938, the school caught fire, and a new four-room building known as Clackamas Elementary was constructed. More rooms were added, but due to continual growth in the area, a new school was built in 1960—Bilquist Elementary, named after Clackamas superintendent Walter Bilquist. (CCHS.)

Clackamas High School (pictured), located on Webster Road near Milwaukie, was dedicated on November 14, 1957. The ceremony took place in the gymnasium with Union High School District superintendent Owen Sabin, principal James Adamson, and rabbi Julius Nodel giving speeches. When it opened, the high school had fewer than 700 students. On April 3, 2002, students moved into the new Clackamas High School building on 122nd Avenue in Clackamas. The opening was delayed from an original 2001 opening date because the building was not ready to be occupied. Almost immediately after the new school opened, portable classrooms were needed to ease overcrowding. Eventually, the nearby Sunrise Middle School was converted into the eastern campus of the high school, and the old Clackamas High School building became Alder Creek Middle School. (MM.)

The Concord School District began in 1856, when families who had recently arrived in the Concord Road area in Oak Grove needed a school. The second Concord School, called the Riverside School, was located near River Road and was in use from 1866 to 1890. This 1886 photograph shows the Riverside School schoolhouse with teacher Neita Barlow (in the plaid dress) standing in the center of the group. (CCHS.)

The third Concord School was a white one-room schoolhouse (at right in this image). It opened in 1890 near SE Concord Road and was in use until the fourth school (at left in the image) was built. The Concord School was named after Concord, Massachusetts, thanks to a suggestion by pioneer William Starkweather. In 1936, the fourth school was torn down, and Concord Elementary School was built; the elementary school closed in 2014. (CCHS.)

Continued enrollment increases at Concord Elementary School made it necessary for a new school to be constructed on River Road in 1955. It was initially called West Concord, but its name was later changed to Riverside Elementary School. This is how the school appeared in 1960. In the 1960s, another school was built on View Acres Road and called View Acres Elementary. (MM.)

In the 1800s, children who lived in Jennings Lodge and Oak Grove attended school in the Concord School District. In 1903, Oak Grove separated from Concord and formed its own district. In 1908, Jennings Lodge did the same and built its own school. This photograph shows the Jennings Lodge School in 1930. (CCHS.)

After Oak Grove formed its own school district in 1903, Oak Grove Grade School was built. This photograph shows how the school appeared in 1920. In 1925, Oak Grove Elementary School opened on Oak Grove Boulevard. The school closed in 2000, and students moved into nearby North Oak Grove Elementary, which then changed its name to Oak Grove. (CCHS.)

On September 9, 1963, Putnam High School opened with 500 freshmen and sophomores. The school district named the school in honor of Dr. Rex Putnam, who served as Oregon Superintendent of Public Instruction from 1937 to 1961. This photograph shows the school library in 1963. In 2003, Putnam High School hosted a forum on the Iraq War with ABC's *World News Tonight* anchor Peter Jennings as moderator. (MM.)

Hector Campbell opened Milwaukie's first school in 1849 and was also its first teacher. The first Milwaukie School District schoolhouse (pictured) was built in the 1850s and was located approximately where Portland Waldorf School now stands along Harrison Street. This schoolhouse was in use until the 1890s, when a new school was built along Main Street where the Milwaukie City Hall would later be constructed. (MM.)

Milwaukie Grammar School, shown here in the 1920s, was built in 1916. Milwaukie students in first through sixth grades moved there from the school that was built in the 1890s. The original building was upgraded over the years and became Milwaukie Elementary School. In 1925, Milwaukie, Clackamas, Oak Grove, Concord, and other grade schools consolidated to form a new high school district called Union. (MM.)

High school education in North Clackamas had a gradual development that stemmed from the desire of school authorities to provide higher education close to home. Union High School District No. 5 was formed by a vote of the people from the districts involved in 1925. The new Milwaukie Union High School was dedicated on September 3, 1926. Milwaukie High School is shown here during Living History Day in 2003. (MM.)

Beginning in 1907, students in Milwaukie received high school instruction at the grade school before transferring and completing their education at a Portland high school. The *Maroon*, the Milwaukie High School annual, was first issued in 1916. North Clackamas School District demolished the old Milwaukie High School in 2018 to make way for a new building. This photograph shows the Milwaukie High School stadium in 1964. (MM.)

On October 20, 1959, Sen. John F. Kennedy addressed a Clackamas County Democratic Party dinner at Milwaukie High School. He returned to Milwaukie in 1960 during his campaign for the Democratic nomination for president of the United States and toured the city, greeted workers at Omark Industries and the Pendleton Woolen Mills, sat at the soda fountain inside Perry's Pharmacy, and gave a speech on American education at Milwaukie High School. His host was Oregon state senator Monroe Sweetland, a leader of Oregon's Democratic Party and a Milwaukie resident. This photograph shows Kennedy with student Pat Honma during the Pledge of Allegiance at Milwaukie High School on April 22, 1960. (MM.)

In 1912, the Ardenwald School District was organized. After Ardenwald was annexed into the Milwaukie School District, Ardenwald Elementary School (pictured) was built in 1924 on Thirty-Sixth Avenue in Milwaukie. After a bond measure passed, a new Ardenwald Elementary School opened in 2010. (MM.)

Here, Ellen "Nell" Martin shows a photograph of the Standard Mill to Ardenwald Elementary School students in 1961. Martin was the daughter of blacksmith shop owner Owen Roberts, and many considered her to be Milwaukie's historian due to her knowledge of the city and collection of historic photographs. Other elementary schools in Milwaukie include Lot Whitcomb (built in 1958), Seth Lewelling (built in 1963), and Linwood (built in 1968). (MM.)

The Wichita School District built the Wichita School in 1909 that is shown in this photograph. The district was named by George Parry, who had formerly lived in Wichita, Kansas. In 1939, Wichita joined the Milwaukie School District, and the Wichita Elementary School opened in 1942. After Wichita Elementary School closed, the Wichita Center for Family and Community opened in its place. (MM.)

After the Harmony School District was organized, the one-room Harmony School was built in 1874. In 1908, a new building was constructed to replace the old school. In 1946, Harmony joined the Milwaukie School District, and a new Harmony Grade School (shown here) opened in 1951. After this school closed in 1988, the Oregon Institute of Technology moved in, followed by Clackamas Community College. (MM.)

A petition to withdraw from the Harmony School District led to the establishment of the Battin School District. Located to the north of Harmony by Battin Road near the Multnomah County border, Battin School was built in 1936. This photograph shows Battin School students in 1953. (MM.)

When it opened, Battin School was a 4-room building, but it eventually expanded into 12 rooms, including a library and a cafeteria. This photograph shows Mrs. Couch's first-grade class at Battin School in 1983. This school closed in 1988. (MM.)

The original Milwaukie Junior High School was built in the 1890s on Main Street in Milwaukie. In 1936, the junior high students moved into a new building on Harrison Street. A time capsule placed at the building in 1936 was opened in 1987 during the celebration of the school's 50th anniversary. This photograph shows the Milwaukie Junior High girls' basketball team in 1932. (MM.)

This picture shows the Milwaukie Junior High School marching band in 1947. The last school year for this junior high was 2001–2002, after which the North Clackamas School District sold the property, and the site became home to the private Portland Waldorf School. (MM.)

Dale Ickes Junior High School (pictured) was built in 1953 along Harmony Road next to the Harmony School. It was originally called Harmony Junior High School but was renamed after Ickes, who had served as superintendent. The school closed in 1990, and students relocated to the new Sunrise Middle School in Clackamas; the Dale Ickes Junior High building then became the Oregon Institute of Technology metro campus. (MM.)

Dale J. Ickes was born in 1903 in Palouse, Washington. He later moved to Oregon and worked as a teacher in St. Helens. In North Clackamas, he served as a school district superintendent for 10 years. He died in 1954, and Harmony Junior High was renamed to honor the man who was known for his efficient administration. Wilbur Rowe Middle School in Milwaukie was also named after a former school superintendent. (MM.)

Milwaukie Elementary School students are shown attending a Veterans Day assembly in this 1991 photograph. In 2003, the El Puente bilingual school opened at Milwaukie Elementary. The North Clackamas School District decided to open El Puente to achieve academic excellence by developing bilingual skills for students who want to learn both English and Spanish. (MM.)

The groundbreaking for Verne A. Duncan Elementary School took place in May 2008. The school, located along SE 172nd Avenue just north of Highway 212 in Happy Valley, was built to relieve crowding at Oregon Trail Elementary in Clackamas. Duncan (fourth from left, with white hair) was a state superintendent of public instruction and an Oregon state senator. (MM.)

Occupational Skills Center

An Invitation To Join. . . . . . . . . .

"A Space Age School With Down to Earth Courses"

14211 S.E. Johnson Rd., Milwaukie, Oregon

CLACKAMAS
MILWAUKIE
REX PUTNAM

Owen Sabin, Superintendent

In the fall of 1967, Union High School District's Occupational Skills Center opened on Johnson Road near Milwaukie. It hosted students from Milwaukie, Clackamas, and Rex Putnam High Schools. This pamphlet was used to promote the skills center. In 1968, McLoughlin Middle School opened nearby. In 2003, McLoughlin Middle closed, and the campuses were renamed the Owen Sabin–Ben Schellenberg Professional Technical Center. Sabin was a former superintendent of Union High School District, and Schellenberg worked as principal at Sunnyside and Linwood Elementary Schools before becoming superintendent of North Clackamas School District in 1980. Altogether, Schellenberg spent 33 years working in the North Clackamas School District. The center was created to provide vocational education in several fields, including law enforcement, building trades, media communications, and others. In 1974, students from the Occupational Skills Center helped to successfully reconstruct the old George Wise house into the Milwaukie Museum. (MM.)

The people gathered here were North Clackamas School District elementary school principals during the 1990–1991 school year. Pictured are, from left to right, (first row) Margaret Bousman, Judy Keeney, Ted Hinds, Lynne Larson, Jim Stell, and Bill Engle; (second row) Kelly Fried, Liz Gill, Barbara Peterson, Roger Capps, Al Fitzpatrick, Gary Salyers, and Terry Spahr; (third row) Ron Orme, Jan Oberg, Gerry Slovil, Dave Larson, Chuck Hopman, and Larry Weber. Since 1971, when the grade school districts of Milwaukie, Concord, Clackamas, and Oak Grove and the Union High School District in Milwaukie unified to create the North Clackamas School District, the region has seen tremendous success in providing efficient and quality education thanks to the district's leadership. In 2017, North Clackamas School District superintendent Matthew Utterback received the National Superintendent of the Year Award from AASA, the School Superintendents Association. (MM.)

*Six*

# WHO'S WHO

Owen Sabin (left), *The Sheriff of Cochise* actor John Bromfield (center), and Clackamas County sheriff Joe Shobe are pictured at a Milwaukie Kiwanis Club show for children in 1958. Sabin was a respected educator who served as superintendent of the Union High School District from 1952 to 1970. Sabin founded the Occupational Skills Center that was later named for him; he died in 1998 in Milwaukie. (MM.)

Arthur Mather (1849–1920) was born in Scotland and immigrated to the United States in 1873. He married Isabel Otty of Mount Scott and settled in Clackamas along the Oregon & California Railroad in 1879. The next year, he was appointed postmaster of the Clackamas post office. Mather's store, post office, and railroad agency were considered the central hub of the Clackamas community. (WGRL.)

Frank Ott (pictured) was born in Wisconsin in 1875 and came to Oregon in 1890. He started a gristmill and general store at the corner of Sunnyside Road and 132nd Avenue that served as the hub of the Sunnyside community during the 20th century. His old mill and store were later repurposed, and the property became known as Sunnyside Commons. (CCHS.)

Ed Rebstock (1911–1984) was a lifelong Happy Valley resident. He is shown here on a tractor during a Happy Valley Park volunteer work day. He helped build many of Happy Valley's roads, strung its telephone lines, installed its water system, organized the fire district, served on the board of directors for the elementary school, worked for the Mount Scott Water District, and was known as Mr. Happy Valley. (HVHC.)

From left to right, Jack Kato, Jim Robnett, Harry Niehoff, and Jack Allen are pictured during a Happy Valley City Council meeting in 1969. At the first city council meeting in 1965, Robnett and Kato tied—with two votes each—in an election among councilmembers for mayor. They used a coin flip to break the tie, and Robnett became mayor and served in that position until January 1995. (HVHC.)

Joseph L. Mumpower, shown here with his wife, Julia (Baxter) Mumpower, was born in 1836 in Virginia. Julia was born in 1840 in Illinois and married Joseph before they headed west and eventually settled in Oregon at the location that would become Carver. Both were popular residents of the community and Clackamas County. (CCHS).

Joseph and Julia Mumpower made their home in Carver on a portion of the Horace and Jane Baker land claim. Their home is shown in this c. 1910 photograph. The Mumpower family established a lumber mill in Carver, and wood from the mill was sold to farmers throughout the area. Joseph and Julia were buried at the Logan Pleasant View Cemetery south of Carver. (CCHS).

Ernest Heinrich (1921–1998) was born in Gladstone. He moved to Carver and worked at the Carver Grade School, then as a dispatcher for Portland Road and Driveway. Heinrich served in the Army during World War II. He was very active in Carver and led the effort to rescue and relocate the German Methodist Church to the Baker Cabin. (CCHS.)

With every gravesite, there is a story. Dee Elliott Wescott was born in Portland in 1927 and moved to Damascus with his family in the 1930s. He founded Wescott's Auto Re-Styling in the 1950s and also volunteered as a firefighter with the Boring Fire District. After Damascus incorporated in 2004, Wescott became the city's first mayor. He died in 2009 and was buried in the Damascus Pioneer Cemetery. (WGRL.)

The Oatfield family home on Oatfield Road is pictured here around 1880. Michael Oatfield was born in 1835 in Austria, and his parents brought him to the United States. He settled in Oregon and purchased the Kellogg donation land claim in Oak Lodge. He married lifelong Oregonian Minerva Thessing, and their farm was regarded as one of the finest in western Oregon. (CCHS.)

Thomas Howell was born in 1842 in Missouri and traveled with his parents across the Oregon Trail to Oregon. His family staked a donation land claim on Sauvie Island along the Columbia River. Howell served as the first postmaster of the Creighton post office in Oak Grove. Thomas and his brother Joseph became noted botanists in the Pacific Northwest, and Thomas wrote *A Flora of Northwest America*. (WGRL.)

When the Clackamas County Historical Society began in the 1950s, each of the founders selected a task to fulfill the society's mission. Wilmer Gardner chose to collect historic photographs. He lived in Jennings Lodge and attended the grade school there as a child. He helped collect thousands of historic photographs from around the county, and the research library at the Museum of the Oregon Territory is named for him. (WGRL.)

William Schindler (center) is shown here with the Milwaukie City Council in 1905. Schindler advocated for Milwaukie to incorporate, as he and other residents were concerned about the storage of gunpowder and other explosives in the city. Schindler worked in construction and real estate development and operated a grocery store on Main Street. After Milwaukie incorporated in 1903, he became the city's first mayor. (MM.)

Florence (Olson) Ledding was born in 1870 in Nebraska. After moving to Oregon, her widowed mother Sophronia married pioneer orchardist Seth Lewelling. Florence passed the Oregon bar, worked as an attorney, and married fellow attorney Herman Ledding. In her will, she left her home to the City of Milwaukie for use as a library. Florence passed away in 1961, and the Ledding Library opened as a memorial to her. (MM.)

William Simon U'Ren was a Milwaukie lawyer when he suffered a severe asthma attack in 1892 and stayed at the home of Seth and Sophronia Lewelling. Their discussions about political reforms led U'Ren to become the father of the Oregon System of the initiative and referendum, giving lawmaking power to the people. His initiative also made Oregon the first state to select US senators by popular vote. (CCHS.)

Dorothy Hester Stenzel was born in 1910 in Milwaukie. As a teenager, she began taking flying lessons from "Tex" Rankin, a Portland stunt pilot, and paid for her lessons by taking parachute jumps. Her daring jumps impressed Rankin so much that she joined his flying circus for a tour across the country and set a world record by performing 56 inverted snap rolls. (MM.)

In 1947, William "Bill" Hupp purchased a photograph studio in the Liberty Theater in Oregon City. In 1958, a fire ravaged the theater building, and Hupp moved his photography studio to Milwaukie. His wife, Ann, worked alongside him until they retired in 1979. In 1974, he was elected mayor of Milwaukie; he served in that role until 1979. This photograph shows Mayor Hupp in a parade in 1978. (MM.)

In the early 1960s, Hurtis Hadley worked as a baker's helper in Portland. He then worked at Albertsons and became the first Black man in Oregon to become a state-certified Journeyman Baker. Hadley eventually left Albertsons, and in 1977, he and his wife, Dorothy, began operating the first Black-owned bakery in Oregon: Milwaukie Pastry Kitchen. This signage was on their delivery vehicle. (MM.)

Bob Moore, pictured with his wife, Charlee, operated a flour mill in California before he moved to Oregon and opened a flour mill on Roethe Road in Jennings Lodge in the late 1970s. In 1988, an arson fire destroyed the building. Moore relocated the flour mill—renamed Bob's Red Mill—to Milwaukie, and he and his store became icons not just in North Clackamas but across the world. (MM.)

This undated photograph (possibly from the 1940s) shows Boy Scouts marching in a parade through Milwaukie. Clair Kuppenbender was a member of the Boy Scouts who became an important part of preserving Milwaukie's history. Kuppenbender was a great orator who provided his experiences of growing up in Milwaukie from the 1930s to the 1950s. The Milwaukie Museum research library is named in his honor. (MM.)

After traveling to California during the Gold Rush, George Wise moved to Oregon and settled in North Clackamas. In 1865, Wise had a home (pictured) built for his family on Lake Road near Milwaukie. In 1973, United Grocers, Inc., donated the house to the Milwaukie Historical Society. Students from the Occupational Skills Center helped the society renovate the house into the Milwaukie Museum, which opened in 1975. (MM.)

This picture is from a July 4th celebration held in Milwaukie in 1905. History is not just about events that happened a long time ago in a place far, far away. History can be something that happened yesterday in one's own hometown. There is much more to history that can be discovered through local historical organizations. In the North Clackamas area, these include the Clackamas County Historical Society, Wilmer Gardner Research Library at the Museum of the Oregon Territory, Milwaukie Museum, Baker Cabin Historical Society, Oak Lodge History Detectives, and Oregon Military Museum at Camp Withycombe. History happens every day. History is remembering. We remember our stories. Our stories emerge from our experiences. Our experiences teach us lessons about life and each other. There is so much history to explore—what are you waiting for? (MM.)

# BIBLIOGRAPHY

Clackamas County Historical Society. *Oregon City Floods*. Charleston, SC: Arcadia Publishing, 2016.

Craven, Richard. *Historic Public Schools of Clackamas County, Oregon*. Oregon City, OR: Self-published, 2017.

Edmunds, Barbara, and Les Lauman. *Milwaukie Then and Now*. Milwaukie, OR: Rowe Junior High School, 1980.

Fegel, Catherine, ed. *The History of Happy Valley, Oregon, 1851–1969*. Portland, OR: Happy Valley School, 1969.

Fourth and fifth grade students. *Clackamas, Oregon II*. Clackamas, OR: Clackamas Elementary School, 1979.

Fourth grade students. *Clackamas, Oregon*. Clackamas, OR: Clackamas Elementary School, 1974.

Hines, Henry Kimball. *An Illustrated History of Oregon*. Chicago: Lewis Publishing Company, 1893.

Kryder, Eleanor. "The Story of Concord School: 1856–1976." Concord Elementary School (1976): 2-3.

Lucia, Ellis. *The Big Blow: The Story of the Pacific Northwest's Columbus Day Storm*. Portland, OR: Overland West Press, 1963.

Lynch, Vera Martin. *Free Land For Free Men: A Story of Clackamas County*. Portland, OR: Artline Printing, 1973.

Maybee, Lottie, and Forest Dale Forbes. *Days and Ways of Old Damascus Oregon*. Calimesa, CA: Damascus Road Press, 1962.

McArthur, Lewis A. *Oregon Geographic Names, 7th Ed.*, rev. McArthur, Lewis L. Portland, OR: Oregon Historical Society Press, 2003.

Olson, Charles Ulaf. *The History of Milwaukie, Oregon*. Milwaukie, OR: Milwaukie Historical Society, 1965.

Parker, David, and Nicole Perry, ed. *History of Education and Schools–Milwaukie, Oregon*. Milwaukie, OR: Milwaukie Historical Society, 2019.

Peterson del Mar, David. *Oregon's Promise: An Interpretive History*. Corvallis, OR: Oregon State University Press, 2003.

# DISCOVER THOUSANDS OF LOCAL HISTORY BOOKS FEATURING MILLIONS OF VINTAGE IMAGES

Arcadia Publishing, the leading local history publisher in the United States, is committed to making history accessible and meaningful through publishing books that celebrate and preserve the heritage of America's people and places.

## Find more books like this at
## www.arcadiapublishing.com

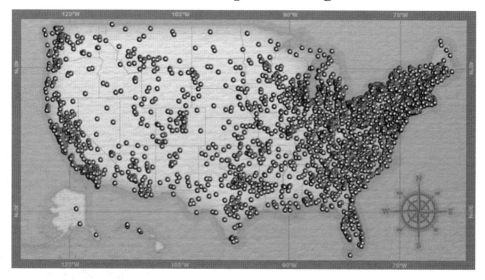

Search for your hometown history, your old stomping grounds, and even your favorite sports team.